Adaptive Programming
Composing Dynamic, Modular Code

Table of Contents

Chapter 1. Introduction

In this Special Report, we delve into the intricate universe of Adaptive Programming: a concept that's shaking up the traditional approach to software development and ushering in a new era of dynamic, modular code. This highly technical subject might seem like attempting to navigate through a foggy abyss for many. However, we illuminate the path and walk you through the fundamental concepts, practical applications, and most importantly, how you can leverage its benefits for better coding. Don't worry, we've managed to distill complex ideas into a simplified narrative that even non-tech savvy readers can absorb. This Special Report is more than just a discussion; it's an invitation to explore the dynamic world of Adaptive Programming and innovate your coding strategies.

Chapter 2. Adaptive Programming: An Introduction

Adaptive Programming is built on the foundation of software development practices, with its roots going deep into tried and tested principles. By providing a flexible strategy to build dynamic and reusable code, it simplifies the coding process and fosters innovation.

2.1. The Fundamental Concepts

Manipulating computers to solve specific problems constitutes the crux of programming. The concept of Adaptive Programming is premised on this very definition. However, it brings an additional dimension — adaptability. The idea is to create such software modules that can adapt to new additions or alterations without any significant rewrites.

This approach results in code that is more flexible and efficient, allowing programmers to add and change functionalities more dynamically. The outcome is that software evolves with needs and demands, without the necessity for large-scale overhauls that can be complex, time-consuming, and costly. In a nutshell, the program adapts without asking for a complete redevelopment cycle.

2.2. The Lego Analogy

To truly understand adaptive programming, it is helpful to liken it to a Lego set. Just as we connect the Lego blocks of different shapes and sizes to craft a structure, Adaptive Programming involves piecing together different modules of code for creating dynamic and evolving software applications. These code pieces can be adapted, modified, or reused as per the specific requirements. Essentially, the Adaptive Programming model ensures that a new change can 'fit in' seamlessly, just as you can always find a place for a new Lego block.

2.3. The Evolution of Coding Paradigms

Programming grew from procedural to object-oriented, and now to adaptive. In the procedural-driven approach, code was written in a top-down linear format, inaugurating a set way of doing things. Next came the Object-Oriented Programming (OOP) focused on creating objects—a data structure encapsulating a set of attributes. While this offered some degree of modularity, there was still a firm blueprint in play.

Adaptive Programming has taken these principles to an entirely new level. Breaking away from traditional constraints, it has codified adaptability, making software more receptive to change. This is a game-changer in the current age, where software ages faster than ever before, and users demand rapid updates and improvements.

2.4. Building Blocks of Adaptive Programming

Understanding Adaptive Programming requires insights into its fundamental components: the dynamic modules. They are essentially individual software components designed to carry out a specific function, encapsulating both the data and the associated behaviours.

These modules are interoperable, which means they can interact smoothly with each other. Interoperability can be of two types: syntactic and semantic. Syntactic interoperability refers to the seamless integration of modules via a common protocol. Semantic interoperability is about conveying and understanding the meaning of the data exchanged between modules.

Another critical aspect is the principle of loose-coupling, wherein each module operates independently of the others. This independence bestows the much-appreciated flexibility upon the software, making the process of modification, addition, or removal of modules a much simpler task.

2.5. Benefits: More than Meets the Eye

Adaptive Programming brings multiple benefits to the table. It facilitates:

1. Quick changes or updates due to its modular approach.
2. Increased coding efficiency due to reduced rewriting needs.
3. High scalability with its adaptive nature.
4. Industry-wide code standardisation since the same modules can be reused in different projects.

This modularity also means that you can improve or correct a particular software feature without disturbing the rest of the code.

2.6. The Journey Ahead: Everyone can Code

By making coding less intimidating and more accessible, Adaptative Programming broadens the appeal of software development. The ability to map out a game plan, adjust it on the fly, and still get to the end goal resonates with everyone.

Adaptive Programming is indeed a valuable tool in today's rapidly evolving landscape. Its benefits are expanding the programming realm, bringing coding within reach of more individuals, promoting collaboration and innovation on an unprecedented scale. By reimagining existing coding paradigms, Adaptive Programming is redefining the future of software development. Adapt and thrive has become the new mantra for success in the coding world.

2.7. Conclusion

As we skim the surface of this vast concept and explore the implications of Adaptive Programming, one thing becomes abundantly clear. Adaptive Programming is creating ripples in traditional coding practices, raising the bar for flexibility, efficiency and innovation in software development.

The potential of this paradigm remains largely untapped. As more people understand and accept Adaptive Programming, it will continue to unlock newer programming tenets, making the creation, management, and modification of software an ever-evolving and exciting journey.

Embracing Adaptive Programming is more than just learning a new coding approach. It is about being prepared for the future, where change is the only constant. In this unpredictable world, Adaptive Programming serves as a beacon guiding programmers towards a future-proof coding strategy.

Chapter 3. From Static to Dynamic: The Evolution of Coding Paradigms

Evolution is the vital force that guides the development of any lifeform. Just as species adapt over time to environmental conditions, so too has coding adapted to the increasing demands and ever-changing dynamics of the computing landscape. In its earliest stage, coding was a static and rigid domain, limited by the constraints of memory, processing power, and programming technology. However, as the digital age progressed the limitations of this paradigm became clear, and a more flexible, dynamic method, adaptive programming, began to emerge.

3.1. Road Through the Historical Lanes

In the wake of World War II, the first programmable, electronic, Turing-complete digital computers were developed. This era was characterized by low-level and extremely static programming methods—mainly assembly language utilized punch cards for coding. Back then, coding was inflexible; even minor changes required exhaustive recoding of entire sections of the system.

The advent of high-level languages (HLL) like COBOL and FORTRAN in the late 1950s introduced a slightly more dynamic system. A slight deviation from the static mold, these languages provided more human-readable code structures with built-in functionality, increasing the programmer's productivity and reducing the occurrence of errors. However, due to their procedural nature, they were often complex, and scalability was a significant challenge.

A revolution came in the early 1960s with the appearance of ALGOL, widely regarded as the first language that allowed structured programming, thus distancing itself from the "spaghetti code" resulting from earlier HLLs. Around the same time, IBM introduced one of the first object-oriented languages, SIMULA. This marked the dawn of a new era in programming, which focused more on the interaction of objects, bringing code closer to a real-world model.

Despite these advancements, the still largely static nature of code during this period necessitated careful planning and significant time investment. Programmers needed to define data types, structures, and algorithms ahead of time, and changes to these aspects could require extensive rework.

3.2. Birth of Modern Dynamic Coding

In the 1980s, the landscape started to shift again with the appearance of modern dynamic languages like Python, Perl, and Ruby. These languages support dynamic typing, meaning they don't require the programmer to specify data type at compile time and can change at runtime, adding a new layer of adaptability to code that directly challenged the static paradigm.

The arrival of object-oriented programming (OOP) further enhanced the dynamism. OOP, with its value placed on classes and objects, facilitated code reusability, inheritability, and encapsulation. Redesiging or modifying a system became simpler, reducing the time and effort required, compared to earlier eras.

Then, Java and C# arrived, bringing with them the concept of "write once, run anywhere," thanks to the JVM and CLR, respectively. This played a significant role in breaking the platform-dependency barrier that static languages struggled to surmount, marking another stride towards the dynamic coding approach.

Scripting languages for web development such as JavaScript, PHP, and later Node.js, emerged, completely discarding the static nature of web pages, and paving the way for more interactive and responsive websites, employing the concept of just-in-time compilation and asynchronous operations.

3.3. Emergence of Adaptive Programming

By the end of the 20th century, Agile methodology began to gain traction, emphasizing continuous delivery, customer feedback, and adaptation over rigid plans. A similar philosophy started to permeate the world of programming with the concept of Adaptive Programming (AP).

AP is all about adapting to changing conditions and requirements. In simpler terms, adaptive programming refers to the practice of writing code that is flexible enough to adapt to changes over time. This shift from a static to dynamic coding paradigm is directly tied to the need for business applications that can adapt quickly to fluctuating customer demands, new regulations, and rapid innovation in technology.

This approach leverages polymorphism and dynamic typing to allow code modules to adjust to different data types and even swap out algorithms dynamically. Patterns like the Strategy Pattern, where algorithms can be selected on the fly, and the Observer Pattern, where objects can subscribe and react to events, are the heart of AP.

Moreover, the principles of AP streamline software development while mitigally lead to code degradation and an increase in bugs. Coupled with the rise of Unit Testing and Test-Driven Development (TDD), AP mitigates these issues by ensuring that code changes do not introduce regressions.

Adaptive programming has truly redefined the boundaries of what it means to write flexible code, ushering in a new era in the realm of application development. Starting as a static, inflexible practice, coding has undergone various shifts before reaching its current dynamic form, embracing adaptability and thriving in ever-changing environments. This evolution has resulted in more resilient, flexible, and future-proof software, capable of tackling challenges yet to be conceived.

Chapter 4. Understanding Modular Code

Modular code is a concept that is fundamental to Adaptive Programming. But what is modular code? Simply put, it's about breaking down a complex problem into manageable pieces. Each of these pieces, or modules, performs a specific function and can be developed, tested, and modified independently from the rest of the codebase. This allows for streamlined collaboration and higher-quality code, facilitating the development of complex software with minimal headaches.

4.1. What Is Modularity and Why Do We Need It?

Modularity is a systemic approach that segments a software system into discrete, manageable, and organized parts called modules. The prime motivation behind creating modular software is the basic human limitation in managing complexity. When creating large systems, our ability to understand and control all aspects at once is challenged.

By dividing tasks into manageable parts, or modules, we can achieve multiple goals. We can understand the functionality of each module, can work on one without needing to understand all the others, and can share tasks among multiple developers. Explicit interfaces define how modules communicate, prevent unwanted side effects and help to control the complexity of the system.

4.2. The Anatomy of a Module

A properly constructed module encapsulates related functions and data, offering a cohesive bundle of functionality. The aim is to create modules that are loosely coupled (little interdependency) and highly cohesive (internal unity or close-knitness of its components).

Each module has an 'interface' and an 'implementation'. An interface is a point of connection between the module and the rest of the system. It defines what functions this module will provide to the system. The implementation is the inner workings of the module, with data and algorithms that provide the functionality promised by the interface. A cardinal rule in modular programming is that modules should communicate exclusively through their interfaces.

4.3. Creating Robust Interfaces

Since modules communicate with the rest of the system via their interfaces, well-designed interfaces are vital for modular programming. They should be clear, stable, minimal, and complete.

- Clear: The interface should be designed so that the user can easily understand it. This often means that the interface design should reflect the user's model of the task, not the programmer's model of the software.

- Stable: A changing interface can cause havoc in a modular system. Once you've established your interface, keep changes to a minimum and thoroughly test any alterations.

- Minimal: The interface should expose only what's needed to perform the module's task. Including unnecessary operations or data can create confusion and increase the likelihood of errors.

- Complete: The interface should provide all the operations a user needs to utilize the module's functionality.

4.4. Advantages of Modular Programming

Modular programming offers several considerable advantages over monolithic programming:

1. Simplicity: Breaking down a large system into smaller components simplifies the program development. Each module is designed to perform a single function, which is simpler to comprehend, develop, and test than a full system.

2. Maintainability: With each module being independent, changing one to fix a bug, upgrade, or add functionality won't affect other modules. This modular isolation lessens the impact of change and makes debugging, updating, and expanding functionality much smoother.

3. Reusability: You can reuse modules, saving time and effort in program design. By creating a library of standard, widely-used modules, you can significantly streamline the coding process.

4. Scalability: Modularity is inherently scalable. If structured well, adding more functions to a system can be as simple as adding new modules.

5. Faster development: With the divide-and-conquer strategy of modularity, multiple developers can work on different modules simultaneously, leading to faster, more efficient development.

4.5. Incorporating Modularity in Software Development

Once you grasp its concept, modular code is relatively simple to integrate into your development workflow:

1. Break down the problem: The first step is to break your problem

into smaller tasks. Any task that makes sense on its own can be turned into a module.

2. Define the interface: Decide what input your module will take and what output it will return. This step is critical to designing a well-functioning, reusable module.

3. Implement the module: Now, you can code the functionality of the module. Remember that the module should function independently of the rest of the system—it's not initially concerned with how other modules will use it, simply with performing its intended task.

4. Test the module: Finally, test the module to ensure it works as intended. Because it's separate from the rest of the system, you should be able to test modules individually.

Remember, modularity isn't rigid. Thinking flexibly about the size and functionality of your modules, balancing depth (how much a module does) with breadth (how many modules you have), will help you create a codebase that's both adaptable and resilient.

Adaptive Programming is driving a revolution in software development, and modular programming is a key part of it. By understanding and implementing modularity, you can future-proof your software, streamline your development process, and increase the quality of your codebase.

Chapter 5. The Framework of Adaptive Programming

Adaptive Programming (AP), in its most fundamental form, is an approach to software development that prioritizes the ability to change. It's about creating flexible, modular software systems that can roll with the punches and fluidly adapt to changing circumstances, requirements and user needs. This principle is fundamental to successful modern software development practices, which increasingly face the challenge of building software for complex, fast-moving and unpredictable environments.

5.1. The Evolution of Adaptive Programming

Evolving from traditional programming paradigms, AP takes a unique "change is constant" approach. It was born out of a necessary shift toward dealing with "wicked problems" - those complex, elusive issues in software development that can't be solved by a standard set of patterns or designs.

Traditional programming often faced difficulties when it came to accommodating changes, especially when they were significant or unforeseen. This rigidity was creating more problems than solutions, forcing developers to spend a great amount of time and resources on rebuilding or altering existing code structures.

AP emerged as an answer to such dilemmas. While incremental changes had been made in the form of object-oriented programming and agile methodologies, the real leap occurred with AP - an approach focused on building software capable of easily accommodating changes, with minimal disruption.

5.2. The Guiding Principles of Adaptive Programming

To understand the framework of AP, let's look at its foundational pillars.

Modularity: One of the key aspects of AP is creating software in discrete, interchangeable 'modules' or components. This results in more maintainable and adaptable systems. Changes in one module don't entail massive ripple effects on the rest of the software, since each module operates independently yet works harmoniously within the larger software ecosystem.

Versatility: AP aims at creating software that can address myriad user needs, across diverse contexts, with the same base code. AP lays emphasis on developing code structures which can inherently handle variability, rather than having to be manually altered constantly by programmers for different scenarios.

Continuous Evolution: AP acknowledges that software will need to evolve continuously to keep pace with rising user expectations and dynamic digital environments. It promotes a mindset of evolutionary development, wherein software is regularly updated, improved, and extended, but on a solid, stable base.

5.3. The Process in Adaptive Programming

The AP process isn't a fundamentally different process from traditional software development. It still follows the classic development phases - requirement gathering, design, implementation, testing, and maintenance. However, the difference is ingrained in how these phases are treated in AP:

Requirement Gathering: Recognizing that user needs are fluid and ever-changing, requirement gathering in AP is seen as an ongoing endeavor rather than a finite phase. Feedback is continuously accommodated, even after the initial launch.

Design: AP encourages designing systems as segments of interchangeable, independent modules. Therefore, alterations can be made to any module without disrupting the overall integrity of the software.

Implementation: Here, AP encourages the use of design patterns and best practices to write clean, maintainable, and modifiable code.

Testing: The AP process foregrounds automated testing. It is crucial to detect errors quickly when the codebase is always evolving.

Maintenance: This is not seen as a 'clean-up' phase but as a continuous evolution and improvement process, building on a stable, reliable core.

5.4. Applying Adaptive Programming

Developers of all experience levels can use the principles of AP to their advantage. For instance, web developers can create modular design components or reusable code snippets that can quickly be adapted to changing user interface requirements.

Similarly, data scientists can build adaptive predictive models – models that automatically fine-tune predictive accuracy over time, learning from the data they ingest.

Moreover, AP shines in software systems that are expected to evolve over long periods of time, adapting to radical changes in user needs, hardware capabilities, or broader digital ecosystems. For example, enterprise resource management software, health informatics systems, or learning management systems, spanning several years and catering to diverse user groups, benefit immensely from the AP approach.

5.5. The Future of Adaptive Programming

Several promising trends are converging to create a future where AP is more crucial than ever before. Advances in machine learning and artificial intelligence technologies are expediently enhancing our ability to create adaptive, learning systems.

Furthermore, the rise of distributed, cloud-based computing architectures provides modern developers with the right platforms to build and deploy resilient, adaptable systems that can meet diverse operational and user needs.

Lastly, the growing focus on user experience places an emphasis on the necessity of fluid, convenient, and adaptive software interfaces. As these trends continue to gather steam, AP will inevitably become the new normal in the realm of programming, making it an essential tool for developers aiming to create the software of the future.

Chapter 6. Building Blocks: Key Components of Adaptive Programming

Adaptive Programming (AP) is a radically different approach to software development. Rather than following the traditional procedural order, this approach enables dynamic interactions and an overall more flexible code structure. To understand this novel idea, we must delve into its building blocks: the components that make AP what it is.

6.1. The Principle of Adaptivity

The fundamental value proposition of Adaptive Programming is its inherent adaptivity. AP operates with the premise that code should be capable of adapting to changing needs. As any programmer can attest, a program's specifications often change throughout its life. The traditional approach of writing rigid code that needs to be rewritten or heavily tweaked each time would be ineffective in such scenarios. AP provides an answer to this predicament with the concept of adaptivity.

In essence, the adaptivity concept allows for automatic rearrangement of parts of the software to accommodate new requirements without necessitating the complete reworking of code. The principle models a program as a collection of many small parts (objects, in most cases) that behave according to rules and messages it produces or receives. The adaptivity ensures that these small parts can be modified, replaced, or rearranged without breaking the entire system.

The advantage of this adaptivity is that it makes the program inherently more robust to changes. It accepts that change is an essential reality of the software life cycle, and rather than fighting it, the program adapted to incorporate it.

6.2. Objects and Messages

Two of the most fundamental components of Adaptive Programming are objects and messages. Like in most object-oriented programming (OOP) paradigms, objects in AP are independent entities with unique properties. Each object has its set of behaviors, defined by methods, and it maintains its state through instance variables.

In Adaptive Programming, systems are modeled as a collection of cooperating objects rather than a sequential flow of instructions. Each object represents an aspect of the problem being solved, which makes the programs more understandable and manageable. Objects interact with each other by sending messages. A message is a command or a request from one object to another to execute a specific method.

This approach makes the system modular and robust. As each object can be independently tested and updated, the system as a whole can better cope with changes.

6.3. Classes and Inheritance

Like OOP, AP uses classes to define objects. A class is basically a blueprint or template for creating objects. Each object created from a class ("an instance of" a class) shares the class' methods and properties.

Adaptive Programming leverages inheritance, a fundamental principle of OOP. Inheritance allows one class to inherit the methods and properties from another class. It provides the ability to create a class hierarchy where a "child" class inherits attributes and behaviors from a "parent" class.

While traditional programming sees code as a rigid structure that is prone to break with changes, AP views code as dynamic entities that can adapt to meet new performance needs. With class inheritance, parent classes can be modified, and those changes propagate through all child classes, thereby achieving adaptability.

6.4. Hot Swapping

One of the major attractions in Adaptive Programming is the concept of hot swapping. Hot swapping refers to the ability to alter system components on the fly while the system continues running. In software development, this could translate to modifying certain parts of code without stopping or restarting the program.

In the ever-growing landscape of software development, where user preferences change swiftly and software updates are inevitable, hot swapping allows developers to upgrade modules, fix bugs, or update functionalities while minimizing system downtime. This leads to seamless user experience and operational continuity, which are vital in today's fast-paced markets.

6.5. Aspect-oriented Programming (AOP)

Adaptive Programming also incorporates aspect-oriented programming. AOP is an approach to programming that aims to increase modularity by separating cross-cutting concerns. These are aspects of a program that cut across its various parts, and changing them in traditional programming models would require changes in multiple places.

AOP allows these aspects to be updated in a single location and have these changes propagate throughout the code. This enhances modularity and reduces the risk and effort associated with implementing changes. As such, AOP is a powerful element of Adaptive Programming, granting it even greater flexibility.

6.6. Conclusion

Adaptive Programming brings a unique perspective to coding. By viewing a program as an ecosystem of interacting objects rather than a static instruction set, AP provides inherent robustness against change. It takes in stride that change is a constant in software development, and rather than fighting it with brittle and rigid code structures, it welcomes it with open arms, offering dynamic, modular code. Adaptive Programming's key components, including objects and messaging, classes and inheritance, hot swapping, and aspect-oriented programming, work collectively to create a paradigm where coding is no longer a fight against change but a symbiotic relationship with it.

With these foundations, you can begin to see how Adaptive Programming could revolutionize the way you approach software development. However, understanding the theory is only the first step. In the following chapters, we will guide you on how to practically implement AP in your own coding endeavors. By truly understanding and implementing these concepts, you can leverage AP to deliver innovative, adaptable software fit for the constantly evolving technological landscape.

Chapter 7. Bringing Adaptivity to Life: Applied Examples

The practice of adaptive programming isn't exactly new, but its full potential has recently been recognized, and it is increasingly on the agenda of innovative coding enthusiasts. This pragmatic approach promotes flexibility in problem-solving and allows for the crafting of effective, efficient, and innovative software. To fully grasp its significance, we need to dive into some concrete examples where adaptive programming practices have been applied to resolve real-world programming issues.

7.1. Modernization of Legacy Systems

Legacy systems are often immovable objects within organizations. They are entrenched, complex, and often built with outdated technology, making them difficult to understand and modify. Traditionally, significant resources were allocated to completely rewrite these systems, often leading to complications due to a lack of understanding of their intricate relationships.

Adaptive programming offers an alternate path. By modeling the target system adaptively, programmers can develop better defined interfaces, which then allow for the gradual replacement of parts of the legacy system. The key here is adaptivity. Changes to the system do not require a complete system overhaul. Instead, as the needs of the business evolve, the modular nature of adaptive programming can help create solutions that can be easily modified.

One spectacular example of this type of application would be the overhaul of banking systems. Many of these systems are decades old, running on mainframe computers. Banks are constantly challenged with evolving demands, necessitating constant changes in their software. Adaptive programming can encapsulate these ever-changing needs in adaptable components, gradually replacing the legacy system with a modern, flexible system.

7.2. Application in AI and Machine Learning

Another intriguing domain where adaptive programming comes into its full swing is in the field of artificial intelligence and machine learning. The inherently dynamic and evolving nature of these disciplines makes them an ideal fit for the adaptive approach.

AI models often need to adapt to new data and conditions. With adaptive programming, the evolving aspects of the models can be encapsulated, making the overall system more adaptable and easier to understand. For instance, Netflix's recommendation engine uses adaptive programming techniques to evolve and refine their recommendation algorithms.

7.3. Advancements in Web Development

Web development constantly involves a struggle against changing user requirements, frequent updates, and relentless competition. Adaptive programming brings agility and dynamic evolution to the field.

For instance, JavaScript frameworks such as React and Angular take an adaptive approach to facilitate modularity, better state management, and easy adaptability to changes in business logic. Separating the UI components and using adaptive programming to manage the state of these components can streamline the process of updating and managing web applications.

7.4. Streamlining Mobile Application Development

Mobile application development has seen a surge in the use of adaptive programming practices. Given the rapid evolution of mobile technologies and user interfaces, creating applications that can withstand drastic changes is essential.

React Native, a popular mobile development framework, utilizes adaptive principles to create components that can be reused and changed as needed. This modular design approach makes it easier to develop applications, as well as to manage and update them as new devices or operating systems appear.

7.5. Reinventing Game Development

Not to forget the gaming industry. Traditional game development may involve enormous amounts of code that can be difficult to manage, adapt, or extend. Here too, adaptive programming steps in to offer innovative solutions.

By building games using adaptive principles, programmers can encapsulate different aspects of the game into detachable modules. This allows easy updates and changes, without affecting the overall game framework. It opens the door to dynamic game development where various components, such as graphics, user interface, and game logic, can evolve separately.

In conclusion, adaptive programming brings to the fore the necessary ability to adapt, evolve, and withstand unpredictable changes in requirements and technologies. Its influence is transformative - from modernizing legacy systems and advancing artificial intelligence to revolutionizing web, mobile, and game development. The principles of adaptivity, modularity, and flexibility it advocates essentially futureproof your coding strategies, all while increasing efficiency and productivity. So, why not take a step towards adaptivity today, and pave the way for software development that's primed for the future?

Chapter 8. The Art of Debugging in Adaptive Programming

Debugging is a critical aspect of the programming process, a truth that spans across all methodologies, languages, and paradicms. Adaptive Programming, despite its dynamic and flexible nature, is not exempt from this necessity. While Adaptive Programming offers a more modular and component-based approach to code construction, it adds its own set of unique challenges when it comes to debugging. From interpreting artifact variation to unveiling hidden dependencies, Adaptive Programming calls for the implementation of innovative debugging strategies to ensure cleaner, error-free code.

8.1. Understanding Debugging in Adaptive Programming

Debugging in Adaptive Programming requires a different perspective than conventional debugging techniques. Due to the dynamic nature of Adaptive Programming, a bug could be originated from various sources such as malware, logic flow issues, complex dependencies, or simply from the often unpredictable interplay of modular components. The nature of Adaptive Programming introduces the need for adaptiveness not just in coding strategies, but also in debugging approaches.

In this paradigm, one not only has to fix possible errors, but also enhance the system's resilience to such bugs in the future by instilling an adaptive, self-correcting behavior where possible. This unique approach of debugging in Adaptive Programming can be summarized in four main steps: identification, isolation, rectification and fortification.

8.2. Bug Identification

The efforts to identify bugs in the Adaptive Programming realm should be as dynamic and versatile as the adaptive code. As this programming paradigm inherently supports modification and evolution, the debugging tools must allow for easy monitoring and interpretation of change, effortlessly detecting deviations from expected outputs or behavior.

Specialized tools like dynamic code analyzers and debuggers that interpret real-time code execution can assist in identifying bugs. Also, creating a culture of frequent, small-scale testing will help to reveal bugs earlier in the development cycle, making them easier to manage and mitigating their impact on the overall project.

8.3. Bug Isolation

Once an anomaly is identified, isolation of the buggy code segment stands as the next challenge. Thanks to the modular and componentized nature of Adaptive Programming, bugs often lie in the maze of interactions among independent components. Hence, the challenge is twofold: figuring out which components are in play and identifying the one causing the issue.

Techniques like boundary value analysis, where the system is tested at the extreme ends of input domains, and error seeding, intentionally introducing bugs to better understand how they behave, can be fruitful here. Crucially, systematic documentation of code interactions, behaviors, and possible pathways also assists in creating a map to navigate the complex structure.

8.4. Bug Rectification

After bug isolation, the next step is bug rectification. It means making changes to the codebase to remove the undesired behavior or output.

The Adaptive Programming's philosophy of continuous change and evolution shines brightly here as rectification often means modifying or replacing the offending module instead of rigorous corrections in the original code.

The fluid nature of adaptive code allows modifications, improvements, and even wholesale replacement of elements to fit the evolving needs of the system. Debugging is no less than coding in this aspect: just like the code adapts, so must the bug fixing strategies.

8.5. Bug Fortification

The last step in the Adaptive Programming debugging loop is fortification. It refers to the process of strengthening the system against similar bugs in the future. Given the predictive, anticipatory nature of Adaptive Programming, fortification could mean devising mechanisms for the system to adapt to similar issues in the future or creating a backstop that switches on when an anomaly like the bug that just got fixed is encountered again.

The idea is to build self-diagnosis and self-healing capabilities into the system. This can be achieved by incorporating analytics, automatic error tracking, or even adaptively self-correcting algorithms into the code.

8.6. Embracing the Art of Debugging in Adaptive Programming

The art of debugging in Adaptive Programming is more than a mechanical process. It's about an enlightened mindset that accepts the subtleties that adaptive code can bring into the debugging process. Breaking down the traditional barrier between coding and debugging, it calls for a novel approach that sees debugging as a core component of the coding and evolution journey.

Empowered with the right strategies to identify, isolate, rectify and fortify, developers can make the most of Adaptive Programming's flexibility and dynamism. As they debug, they don't just fix issues, they contribute to the code's continued adaptation, evolution, and improvement over time, bringing out the true potential of Adaptive Programming.

Remember, in Adaptive Programming, debugging is not a roadblock, it's a stepping stone to greater adaptability and resilience. Embrace it, and let your code not just survive, but thrive amid changes.

Chapter 9. Adaptive Programming: The Risks and Challenges

Adaptive programming, despite all its positives, is not without its share of challenges and risks. Very much like any other paradigm shift, it brings with it certain reservations among programming veterans and enthusiasts. The challenges with adaptive programming stem primarily from its dynamic nature that makes system and program predictability hard to achieve without a comprehensive understanding of the paradigm.

9.1. Understanding the Complexity

Adaptive programming often demands an entirely new mindset to viscerally understand and design complex and tangled systems. Designing adaptive systems requires the ability to abstractly, and rather dynamically, think about how software entities interact with one another. For instance, managing changing relationships among OO (object-oriented) components can be challenging for many programmers used to the traditional linear view of systems.

Problems become more pronounced when programmers need to manipulate existing code. Often, making changes in one system or a component can have a ripple effect and cause unforeseen issues in seemingly unrelated parts of the code. Every code modification may result in unintended modifications in behaviours which could be challenging to debug later.

9.2. Adaptive Programming and The Learning Curve

One of the higher hurdles with adaptive programming is undoubtedly the steep learning curve. As a programmer, you are required to wear different hats – evolving from being just a coder to being a "literal" system designer. Mastering adaptive programming requires understanding complex topics like aspect-oriented programming, OOP, entity component systems, and system-based design.

This demand for broad and deep knowledge could discourage many from pursuing or implementing adaptive programming, leading to a slower adoption rate which is a challenge in itself. Moreover, finding comprehensive and beginner-friendly resources for learning adaptive programming could be another hurdle.

9.3. Necessity for High-Level Design

With adaptive programming, the need for high-level system design can't be overstated. Although the paradigm promotes regular change and adaptability, programmers still need to have a blueprint for their software or system. But creating this blueprint is a challenging task that requires skill and experience.

A poorly designed adaptive system can quickly end up as an unmanageable maze of adaptive components, making it tough to locate erroneous behaviours. Hence, designing at a high level, while maintaining the understanding of the system's invariant properties, makes adaptive programming an intricate task for the uninitiated.

9.4. The Challenge of Predictability

When using traditional programming methods, programmers can

predict and foresee the outcomes of their codes to a good extent. However, this is not the case with adaptive programming.

Due to the sophisticated interplay between components, predicting the outcome of a code snippet is tricky and often impossible without a sound understanding of the entire system. This uncertainty is compounded by the component interactions' dynamic nature, creating gargantuan predictability challenges.

9.5. Testing and Debugging Woes

Testing and debugging codes in adaptive systems is another setback. Traditional approaches like unit testing are not very effective here due to the broad influences that one component can have. Hence, even an isolated unit test can give a green signal to a potentially faulty code.

Debugging also presents problems because of the growing complexity of software systems. Symptoms of a software bug often become noticeable far from the root cause, making the debugging process more complicated.

9.6. The Risk of Overcomplication

Given the freedom adaptive programming offers, there's an inherent risk of overcomplication. Programmers might be tempted to create overly complex designs with unnecessary adaptive features that do not add any substantial functionality to the software. This can lead to extra expenditure of time and resources, thus hindering productivity.

In conclusion, adaptive programming, though a powerful paradigm shift in the software industry, is not without its pitfalls. Understanding these challenges is crucial for smooth and effective implementation of adaptive programming practices. By mastering these risks, programmers can fully leverage the dynamic power of adaptive programming to create better software solutions.

Chapter 10. Future Trends in Adaptive Programming

We stand at the cusp of another revolution in the realms of software development. Looking at recent advancements, we're witnessing the dawning of several exciting new trends that promise to substantially shape Adaptive Programming's future.

10.1. Shifting Landscape: Enhanced Modularity and Flexibility

The modular structure has been an inherent attribute of Adaptive Programming. However, we can expect these modular characteristics to be enhanced in the future. They not only allow code pieces to be assembled like building blocks, fitting perfectly into the desired structure, but they are also poised for autonomous adaptation. Picture this: Code modules independently updating based on identified usage patterns, adopting changes, and resolving inconsistencies without human intervention!

This shift will lead to profound changes in the approach to software development, focusing more on managing the interactions between these modular entities rather than worrying about the low-level details of their implementation. This is akin to being the conductor of an orchestra, directing and modulating the symphony, rather than playing each instrument oneself.

We can also expect flexibility to increase. In the context of Adaptive Programming, flexibility means adapting to changes with minimal human input. Consider an application capable of learning the changing user behaviors and modifying its responses suitably. As we move towards more complex systems, this kind of adaptability is not just desirable but absolutely necessary.

10.2. Artificial Intelligence and Machine Learning Integration

The merge of Adaptive Programming with Artificial Intelligence (AI) and Machine Learning (ML) has great potential in transforming the face of modern software. AI and ML enable the decision-making process to be automated. Essentially, they enable software to "learn from experience" and adapt its behavior appropriately.

Furthermore, AI-enabled Adaptive Programming will optimize code performance by recognizing patterns, implementing best practices, and predicting issues before they occur. Advanced AI models can proactively shape programs based on the incoming data, improve the logic behind code modifications, and make more intelligent decisions regarding runtime behaviors and fault handling.

10.3. Rise of Quantum Computing

Quantum computing is reimagining the traditional definition of computing power. Utilizing quantum bits, or qubits, they offer exponential processing capabilities. But quantum mechanics also introduce uncertainties leading to more trial-and-error solutions increases. Consequently, the need for more adaptive programs will rise – ones that can effectively handle the quantum environment's unpredictability, run multiple solutions simultaneously and dynamically select the best one based on the outcomes.

10.4. Adaptation at Different Abstraction Levels

In the future, we might witness adaptive behaviors implemented at various abstraction levels. Currently, Adaptive Programming is mostly prevalent at high abstraction layers in application and services terrain. There will likely be a push to incorporate adaptive behaviors in the lower abstraction levels, such as operating systems and middleware, to better accommodate the needs of adaptive applications. Such inclusion will significantly impact system-level resource allocation strategies, security protocols, and privacy issues.

10.5. Greater Security and Robustness

With the increasingly volatile cyber scenario, adaptive programs will be indispensable in mitigating cyber threats dynamically. They will be able to real-time adapt to different attack strategies and update their protective measures as per the ongoing threat landscape. Imagine a system that learns from each attack strategy it faces, thus significantly improving its robustness.

In conclusion, adaptive programming is a fascinating domain, and it has the potential to revolutionize the way software is developed and used. Advances in AI, an increased understanding of abstraction levels, and the integration of adaptive programs in quantum computing, represent just a glimpse of the future for adaptive programming. The trends indicate that we are entirely on track to tackle the challenges of a dynamic and volatile world in the ever-shifting landscape of computer science and technology.

Chapter 11. Stepping into the Future: Developing Your Own Adaptive Code

Adaptive Programming presents us with an intriguing approach to software development. To delve deeper and understand more about it requires a step-by-step deconstruction of its theory and practice. Before initiating this journey of comprehension, recognizing one essential truth is pivotal: like all evolution, adaptive programming is not an overnight burst but a result of gradual, careful progression.

11.1. Theoretical Framework

Adaptive Programming, by its very core, is a profound rebellion against static, immutable code. It seeks an alternative path where code plays the roles of both the creator and its creation, directly questioning the conventional wisdom that code should serve a single, predetermined role during its lifecycle.

In essence, Adaptive Programming is a subset of a broader subject, that of Adaptive Systems. Adaptive systems learn and adapt to their environments, finding the most suitable responses to eventualities. Looking at code through this particular lens, we see it evolving to respond to changing circumstances without the outright need for constant developer involvement.

One component of adaptive systems is called learning algorithms, which adjust their behavior based on data over time. For instance, machine learning algorithms like neural networks are famous examples of these. But Adaptive Programming doesn't stop there. It bridges the space between simple adaptive systems, like the classical machine learning examples, and self-sufficient code, which can make elaborate changes to its structure and functionality.

11.2. Designing Adaptive Code

The step from theory to practice involves designing your own adaptive code. It starts with choosing an appropriate language that support features suitable for Adaptive Programming. Scripting languages like Python or Lua can be exceptionally suited due to their dynamic nature. However, it's important to note that language selection is just the tip of the iceberg. A critical aspect lies in pattern selection.

Patterns are the repeated coding paradigms which we use to solve common problems. Understanding the Adaptive Programming approach requires us to understand some famous patterns, such as the Strategy Pattern or the Observer Pattern.

1. **Strategy Pattern**: This pattern defines a series of algorithms, encapsulates each one and makes them interchangeable. It lets the algorithm change independently from the clients that use it.

2. **Observer Pattern**: A subject maintains a list of its dependents, called observers, and notifies them automatically of any state changes.

These patterns facilitate the behavior of the code to change at runtime.

11.3. Hands-On Coding

With an understanding of patterns, we now delve into writing adaptive code. Let's start with an example in Python.

```python
class Strategy(object):
    def __init__(self, func=None):
        self.name = "Default Method"
        if func is not None:
```

```python
        self.execute = func

    def execute(self):
        print("{} is used!".format(self.name))

strategy0 = Strategy()
strategy0.execute()

def strategy_one():
    print("Strategy One!")

strategy1 = Strategy(strategy_one)
strategy1.name = "Strategy One"
strategy1.execute()
```

This Python script uses the Strategy pattern to change functionality at runtime. Initially, the "Strategy" class has an "execute" method that prints a particular statement. When creating an instance of the "Strategy" class, we can redefine its "execute" method. This way, we're bending the code to fit our needs at runtime, invoking adaptability.

11.4. Adaptive Programming & AI

The fine line between Adaptive Programming and Artificial Intelligence (AI) is increasingly narrowing as both address dynamic behavior. AI, specifically Machine Learning (ML) incorporates adaptability as a fundamental aspect where the ML model trains on provided data and uses extracted patterns to process new data.

Adaptive Programming can integrate with AI to predict behavior. For example, knowing that tomorrow is a holiday, an adaptive weather application might be programmed to give more information about outdoor activities instead of just temperature and humidity levels.

11.5. Pitfalls and Precautions

Adaptive Programming opens up doors for innovative applications. However, it's vital to exercise caution. Since adaptive code inherently involves uncertainty, it might behave unexpectedly in some situations. Thorough testing is significantly important to ensure that it's reliable and won't cause undesirable consequences. Code maintainability is another challenge as living code bases require a constant monitoring mechanism.

11.6. Conclusion

Adaptive Programming offers a unique window into the future of software development. It reshuffles the fundamental thought process about programming and code's static nature. As we continue to evolve our understanding of this innovative methodology, remember: the complexities of today are the simplicities of tomorrow. By accepting the challenge, you are not only stepping into the future but also becoming instrumental in shaping it.

www.ingramcontent.com/pod-product-compliance
Lightning Source LLC
Chambersburg PA
CBHW071012260726
48661CB00007B/2911